CELEBRATE THE UNITED STATES!

WHY DO WE HAVE NATIONAL PARKS?

BY BEATRICE HARRIS

Gareth Stevens PUBLISHING

Please visit our website, www.garethstevens.com. For a free color catalog of all our high-quality books, call toll free 1-800-542-2595 or fax 1-877-542-2596.

Library of Congress Cataloging-in-Publication Data
Names: Harris, Beatrice, author.
Title: Why do we have national parks? / Beatrice Harris.
Description: New York : Gareth Stevens Publishing, [2026] | Series: Celebrate the United States! | Includes bibliographical references and index.
Identifiers: LCCN 2024059390 (print) | LCCN 2024059391 (ebook) | ISBN 9781482471090 (lib. bdg.) | ISBN 9781482471083 (paperback) | ISBN 9781482471106 (ebook)
Subjects: LCSH: National parks and reserves–United States–Juvenile literature.
Classification: LCC E160 .H374 2026 (print) | LCC E160 (ebook) | DDC 917.3–dc23/eng/20250220
LC record available at https://lccn.loc.gov/2024059390
LC ebook record available at https://lccn.loc.gov/2024059391

Published in 2026 by
Gareth Stevens Publishing
2544 Clinton Street
Buffalo, NY 14224

Designer: Jeffrey Taylor
Editor: Therese Shea

Photo credits: Series art (blue background) Paladin12/Shutterstock.com; Cover, p. 1 f11photo/Shutterstock.com; p. 5 Rolf_52/Shutterstock.com; p. 7 KGphoto91/Shutterstock.com; p. 9 Framalicious/Shutterstock.com; p. 11 Joseph Sohm/Shutterstock.com; p. 13 BlueBarronPhoto/Shutterstock.com; p. 15 tsuchi/Shutterstock.com; p. 16 (inset) Aleksandr Lupin/Shutterstock.com; p. 17 Zack Frank/Shutterstock.com; p. 19 Kris Patrick/Shutterstock.com; p. 21 Limolida Design Studio/Shutterstock.com.

Printed in the United States of America

CPSIA compliance information: Batch #CS26GS: For further information contact Gareth Stevens at 1-800-542-2595.

CONTENTS

Boldface words appear in the glossary.

Preserved

Do you like plants and animals? Do you enjoy beauty in nature? You can find all of these in a national park. These are places set aside by the U.S. government to **preserve** the **resources** found within them.

YELLOWSTONE
NATIONAL
PARK
NATIONAL
PARK
SERVICE

National parks become **federal** land. This means the federal government owns it. The federal agency called the Department of the Interior oversees it. No one can buy the land, build on it, or change it in any way without the federal government allowing it.

NATIONAL
PARK
SERVICE
Department
of the Interior
CANYONLANDS
NATIONAL PARK
UNITED STATES DEPARTMENT OF THE INTERIOR
NATIONAL PARK SERVICE

The First

In 1872, Yellowstone National Park in today's Wyoming, Montana, and Idaho became the first U.S. national park. Congress set aside the park for "the **benefit** and enjoyment of the people" of the United States. It was the first national park in the world!

hot spring in Yellowstone National Park

Now Many

As of 2024, the United States has a large national park system of over 400 areas. Just 63 of these areas are called national parks. Only Congress can create new national parks. It also created the National Park Service to care for the parks.

Bryce Canyon Map and
Bryce Canyon

For Protection

National parks help protect animals, plants, and their **habitats**. The National Park Service only allows a certain amount of building and activity. It may even close areas within a park to make sure a species, or kind of plant or animal, **survives**.

bears in Grand Teton National Park, Wyoming

Protecting Culture Too

National parks also protect areas with **cultural** importance. Mesa Verde National Park in Colorado protects the **ancient** dwellings, or homes, of the Ancestral Puebloan people. These cliff homes were built more than 700 years ago! Visitors can learn about these ancient people and their culture at the national park.

A New National Park

In 2021, Congress established a new national park in West Virginia. New River Gorge National Park and Preserve contains one of the oldest rivers on the **continent**. It runs through deep **canyons**. Visitors can do many activities there, such as rock climbing, hiking, and white-water rafting.

white-water rafting

Park Rules

While national parks are for people's enjoyment, all have their own rules to follow. The parks ask people not to leave their trash or feed wild animals. It's also important to stay on trails and out of marked areas. Following rules helps protect wildlife and visitors.

Help Us Protect
Fragile Plants
Please
Stay on
Designated
Trails

Many Parks, Many Visitors

More than 330 million people visit national parks each year. Most parks ask for a fee to enter, which helps the park service care for the trails and buildings. The national parks provide so many **opportunities** to learn and have fun. Which park would you like to visit?

Know More National Parks

Name	Where It Is
Denali	Alaska
Grand Canyon	Arizona
Death Valley	California, Nevada
Yosemite	California
Everglades	Florida
Acadia	Maine
Great Smoky Mountains	North Carolina, Tennessee
Big Bend	Texas
Olympic	Washington
Glacier	Montana

GLOSSARY

ancient: From a very long time ago.

benefit: A helpful or good effect.

canyon: A deep valley with steep sides.

continent: One of Earth's seven great landmasses.

cultural: Having to do with the beliefs and ways of life of a group of people.

federal: Having to do with the national government.

habitat: The natural place where an animal or plant lives.

opportunity: A time in which something can be done.

preserve: To keep safe. Also, a place set aside for animals and plants.

resource: A usable supply of something.

survive: To live through something.

FOR MORE INFORMATION

BOOKS

Anderson, Daisy. *Yosemite National Park*. New York, NY: Crabtree, 2023.

Walton, Kathryn. *Visit Yellowstone National Park!* New York, NY: Enslow Publishing, 2024.

WEBSITES

National Geographic: National Parks
www.nationalgeographic.com/travel/national-parks
Find amazing pictures of the national parks here.

National Park Service
www.nps.gov/index.htm
Learn more about the parks and the people who care for them.

Publisher's note to educators and parents: Our editors have carefully reviewed these websites to ensure that they are suitable for students. Many websites change frequently, however, and we cannot guarantee that a site's future contents will continue to meet our high standards of quality and educational value. Be advised that students should be closely supervised whenever they access the internet.

INDEX